Literacy Ce[nters]

for the Middle Grades

Literacy Centers
for the Middle Grades

Dot Walker • **Terry Davidson**

⊶ **Dominie Press, Inc.**

Published in the United States of America by:

Dominie Press, Inc.

1949 Kellogg Avenue
Carlsbad, California 92008 USA
www.dominie.com

ISBN 0-7685-0469-4
Printed in Hong Kong
1 2 3 4 5 6 PH 06 05 04

Contents

AN INTRODUCTION TO LITERACY CENTERS

In early childhood classrooms, literacy centers have evolved as part of the balanced literacy planning approach, where students learn a range of literacy concepts in order to learn how to read, view, write, listen, and speak for a variety of purposes and audiences. The establishment of literacy centers within the classroom enables the freeing up of the teacher to provide focused and explicit teaching episodes with small groups of students or individuals – for example, during guided reading. In this way, all students benefit as they all receive focused teacher attention on a regular basis, primarily in a small group situation. The students' needs and the teacher's management style will affect the organization of the groups.

In the middle to upper elementary years, the concepts developed in the early years are extended and developed, involving a greater degree of cognitive analysis about texts and how they work. Students move from a phase of learning "how to" read, view, write, listen, and speak to a phase of reading, viewing, writing, listening, and speaking "to learn." Many of the strategies that have proven successful in the early years are equally successful in the middle and upper elementary years. The establishment of literacy centers as part of a balanced literacy approach supports students' continuing literacy development, with each center containing materials to teach, reinforce, and consolidate to enrich skills and develop concepts. Independence and risk-taking are encouraged, with students taking increased responsibility, and opportunities are provided to further build cooperative and social learning skills among the students.

Successful implementation of literacy centers doesn't just happen. There are several important considerations to be taken into account. The establishment of a workable physical environment, organization of resources, planning for learning, assessment, and timetabling are all vital to the management of literacy centers within the classroom.

It is important that there is a clear purpose, and that the learning activities are carefully planned with a clear understanding of the standards and expected outcomes, taking into consideration the developmental needs of the learners. Oral language development is embedded in the literacy center tasks.

In establishing the physical environment, it is necessary to consider the movement of students, noisy and quiet areas, spatial requirements for particular activities, visibility of students, and ease of access to materials and resources required.

The resources used in the centers must be durable. They may be commercially produced or teacher-made, and will include the whole of the classroom environment, as this is a valuable resource for a number of activities. In addition to being good models for the students, the resources must meet their developmental needs. Open-ended tasks and resources ensure that they are reusable and cater to a diverse range of student abilities. Using a range of tasks that cater to diversity in students' learning styles is also important in order for all students to develop and achieve success.

Children need to have literacy center activities introduced to them before they can be expected to engage effectively with them in collaborative groups or independently. Routines and rules for use need to be clearly defined and established. If computer software is being used, it is necessary for the students to be familiar with how to use it, and to have had ample prior exposure to it before they are expected to work independently. Students can be directed to an activity or task through the use of a task board or literacy center task chart. These can also assist with the establishment of expectations and routines, particularly for students who are not accustomed to working independently or interdependently.

Literacy centers can, however, be organized in a number of ways. Students may rotate between activities as directed by the task board, self-select activities from those available, or work on a group or individualized contract. Contracts are particularly suited to older students, requiring them to manage their time effectively. The tasks to be completed and the time frame for completion can be negotiated between the teacher and the students in the class.

Management of the classroom has to be flexible and responsive to students' needs. The use of flexible groupings is an important aspect in the establishment of literacy centers, as it enables maximization of teaching and learning opportunities. The learning outcomes for either individual or small groups of students working in a center should be clearly identifiable.

It is important to plan for a sharing or discussion time at the end of the literacy center time. This validates the independent activities that the students have been engaging in, and provides an opportunity for the teacher to monitor work and give the students appropriate praise and feedback. It encourages others to appreciate the efforts of their classmates and enables them to engage in the giving and receiving of constructive criticism. This time also provides for meaningful and purposeful opportunities to engage students in using oral language skills. During this time, students are reminded that they are expected to participate and engage effectively in literacy center tasks and may be called upon to provide feedback or to produce something to be shared. This sharing time may take a variety of forms, such as whole group, or a strategy such as "think, pair, share." In this way, teachers are also establishing a warm and supportive environment that enhances learning and acknowledges differences in students' needs and abilities.

Assessment and evaluation are essential elements in any classroom. It is important that at the beginning of the year, particularly if you are working with a new group of students, that some form of initial assessments is undertaken. This will be invaluable for effective planning and preparation for establishing literacy centers as part of the whole literacy program.

It is important that teachers employ a variety of formal and informal assessment strategies in order to establish this baseline for planning. Ongoing tracking will enable the teacher not only to monitor and assess student progress, but also to evaluate the effectiveness of the learning activities and environment as part of the literacy program.

ADVANTAGES OF USING LITERACY CENTERS

- Literacy centers play an important role in helping students become fluent readers and writers.

- They form part of a balanced literacy program, which includes modeled, shared, guided, and independent teaching and learning strategies.

- Literacy strategies and behaviors are reinforced, and opportunities are provided to practice and consolidate skills and understandings.

- Literacy centers include structured activities where students practice literacy strategies collaboratively and independently, while teachers observe, monitor, teach, and/or assess.

- Literacy centers provide opportunities for students to use their imagination and develop their problem-solving abilities.

- Activities, targeted at a range of ability levels, enable students to practice and consolidate a variety of skills.

- Literacy centers provide purposeful and interactive activities that challenge the learner.

- Literacy centers are well organized and predictable, and they have clearly defined expectations that assist children in managing their time and behavior.

- Literacy centers provide opportunities for flexible groupings of students.

- Literacy centers minimize preparation time.

- Literacy centers provide opportunities for engagement in meaningful activities related to familiar modeled, shared, and guided texts used in the classroom.

SOME OTHER POINTS TO CONSIDER

Literacy center activities always need to be explicitly modeled, explained, monitored, and debriefed.

Teachers are required to carefully consider resources and materials used, particularly texts for cultural and linguistic content, considering the relevance of context, and avoiding materials with stereotyping and bias.

Time needs to be built into the teacher's planning so that experiences, ideas, and work arising from literacy centers can be shared with the whole class. It is this peer modeling that encourages all students to continue to engage in the literacy centers.

Students need to know what to do, once they have completed work in a center and also where to put any work they may have completed. One idea is for each student to have a literacy center notebook or folder where written work is kept. This also provides a record for the teacher of the literacy centers each student has been involved in.

Teachers need to assess the cooperative, social, and task skills of their students before introducing literacy centers. Some aspects of student behavior that may need to be explicitly taught are:

- using quiet voices
- using people's names
- taking turns
- completing a task
- sharing resources
- listening to others
- staying with your group or partner
- problem solving
- constructive criticism

It is important to begin slowly when first introducing the concept of literacy centers to a class. Set up only one or two centers to begin with. Small groups of students are then sent to work in the centers for a given time. During this time the teacher remains with the rest of the class. When the allocated time is up, the groups are brought back and are given feedback on how they worked at the center. At this time the groups can also give their own feedback to each of their group members about how they worked as part of the group.

This process can be repeated the following day with different groups of students as the teacher slowly builds on the number of literacy centers offered. This procedure may seem very time-consuming, but by moving students slowly toward working independently and interdependently, a teacher will ensure success in implementing literacy centers as an effective component of a successful literacy program.

PROCEDURE

It is important that the class has ownership of the book center and that teachers involve students in the planning, setting up, and daily organization of the center.

Discussions should take place on a regular basis. These discussions should focus on:

- expectations for behavior in the center
- changing and arranging reading materials
- promoting popular books by either "show and tell" or posters
- when and who uses the center

Following are three examples of charts that could be included in a reading center.

OUR TOP TEN BOOKS FOR THIS MONTH

(These can be listed following a class voting session.)

GUIDELINES FOR USING THIS BOOK CENTER

- Move quietly in the center.
- Do not disturb other people.
- If you can't find the book you are looking for, make a second choice.
- Handle books carefully.
- Make sure you have clean hands.
- Keep the bookshelves tidy.

THE DIFFERENT TYPES OF BOOKS IN OUR CENTER

- Information books
- Picture books
- Historical fiction
- Fantasy
- Folktales
- Plays
- How to … books
- Biographies
- Autobiographies

The above could be displayed as a chart, with students recording the books they have read by genre rather than title.

PURPOSE

- To expose students to a wide variety of reading materials and to develop attitudes in students that reading is not only an enjoyable experience, but also a means of locating information.

OVERVIEW

At different times during each day, students will access the reading center for a variety of purposes. This will be organized through the classroom teacher's daily literacy planning. For example, a small group of students could work in the center researching information, or all students in the class could choose some reading material from the center for an independent reading session.

MATERIALS

- A wide selection of reading materials that encourage students to spend time in the center reading. The students' interests and their reading ability will dictate this. The center should contain quality books and other reading materials, such as:

  - magazines
  - newspapers
  - student/class-made books
  - school newsletters
  - photograph albums
  - catalogs
  - comic strips
  - program guides

- Comfortable seating, such as bean bags or cushions, should also be made available.

PURPOSE

- Students will be able to evaluate and assess their own reading progress.

OVERVIEW

Students use journals to reflect on the books they have read. This provides a record for teachers, parents, students, and support staff.

MATERIALS

- A small notebook or journal

PROCEDURE

- Demonstrate and model the use of the journal.

- Discuss your expectation of how and when students will work on their journals.

- All journal entries should be dated, and teachers should ask students to share an entry of their choice with the class on a regular basis.

- A list of questions can provide support for students who may require this.

A highly successful strategy that encourages students to use journals is for the teacher to write responses to the students' comments. This can lead to ongoing written interactions about a text, especially if questions are asked. The journal can be used as a guide for the teacher when conferencing or planning small focused teaching groups in the area of reading.

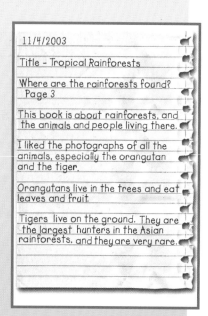

◀ **This sample journal entry is based on a reading of *Tropical Rainforests*, written by Alison Ballance and published by Dominie Press.**

POSSIBLE QUESTIONS

- What did you like best about the book?
- What did you think about the setting?
- Did the photographs fit with the text?
- Were the photographs informative?
- What did you learn from this book?
- Have you read any other books by this author?
- How would you rate this book on a scale of 1 to 10?
- Did you like the end of the book?
- Write three sentences explaining what happened in the beginnning, the middle, and the end of the book.

PROCEDURE

As students enter the middle grades, many of them will be well on their way to becoming independent writers. As teachers, it is therefore important that we provide as many opportunities as possible for students to write and publish their own work.

However, there is still a need for teachers to plan writing workshops, where small groups or whole classes of students have direct teaching about specific aspects of written text.

The teaching focus of these workshops is dictated by three main issues:

- the observed developmental needs of the students
- the school writing curriculum and expectations of genres to be taught
- the interests of the students

If a new genre is introduced to the class, examples of it will need to be displayed on a large chart so that the structure of the genre can be used by students as a reference.

The genres taught should reflect the purposes of the text, the audience, and the interests of the students. Some common genres that are usually taught in middle grades are:

- procedures
- reports
- explanations
- expositions
- narratives
- visual texts, such as comic strips/cartoons/web pages/e-mails

The use of tape recorders for students to plan and verbalize their ideas prior to writing provides a supportive scaffold. In this way, students' ideas are recorded without their having to be concerned with the mechanics of writing.

It is not essential that students go through the entire writing process every time they write. Teachers should expect students to publish a piece of work (depending on the length) perhaps once every two weeks.

Once the writing center has been established, a teacher can work with a smaller group of students on a specific skill or process while a group is working in the center.

PURPOSE

Through a class writing center, students are provided with an opportunity to practice and consolidate their writing skills and understandings for a range of purposes and audiences.

Establishing flexible, exciting, and interesting writing centers provides opportunities for students to be actively engaged in making decisions and taking responsibility for their writing.

Opportunities to write should encourage both independent and cooperative task management engagement.

OVERVIEW

Organization of a writing center in the classroom enables flexible use by individuals or small groups of students with varied levels of ability. The center provides opportunities for students to plan, edit, consolidate, and publish their writing in a variety of forms using a variety of mediums. The teacher's planning and organization will provide opportunities for focused observation of students or conferencing with individuals or small groups of students working at the writing center.

MATERIALS

- A variety of writing materials, paper, and cards

- A computer for researching, drafting, and publishing students' work

- Folded cards and small made-up blank books

- A utility box containing staplers, scissors, clips, rubber bands, sticky notes, tape, a date stamp, and hole punches

- A selection of dictionaries and thesauruses

- A "Have a go" book where students can try to spell words before checking for the correct spelling

- Editing and proofreading guides

- Punctuation charts

- Grammar guides

- Guides and examples for the range of genres that the students have been exposed to

- Plastic sheet protectors or individual folders in which to keep drafts of work

- A box containing stimulus pictures based on the interests of the class

- Writing support charts, such as *Who, What, When, Where, Why,* and *Feelings*

It is important for teachers to acknowledge that many students need a rehearsal time prior to the writing process. This can take the form of:

- drawing

- discussing

- using a cognitive organizer, such as a character web or snapshot diagram

- visualizing

- note-taking

One-to-one or small group conferencing can be carried out by the teacher during the writing process. This is where a teacher is able to see the specific assistance students require to become independent editors of their written work. Most teachers organize this on a rotational basis, conferencing with three to four students each day.

It is also important to provide time for sharing students' writing. This often gives other students ideas and motivation for further writing.

Students' writing must be valued and either displayed or (if student-made books) made part of the class reading materials.

Some successful writing activities that are both purposeful and motivating are:

▲ **Talking about writing and the importance of research**

- students writing books for younger students

- penpal writing, where letters are written to a class in a different country

- planning a school event – writing invitations, programs, menus, etc.

- movie or video reviews

- writing to movie or sports personalities

- writing and producing a class newspaper

PROCEDURE

Mind maps take a variety of shapes and forms. The most common has branches coming out from a central title.

To begin a mind map:

- Start with a central title or key point in the middle of the page.
- Draw a line for each key word or heading. Consider creative use of line styles.
- Write a key word or simple phrase for each line.
- Use lower case print for clarity.
- Drawings, arrows, symbols, highlighters, and colors add to the uniqueness of mind maps.

Mind maps should be working documents that are refined and reviewed in order to further develop ideas.

Mind maps can be used individually or in groups:

- to summarize information
- as a note-taking method
- to record brainstormed ideas and information
- to plan prior to writing
- to organize thoughts
- to plan for oral presentations
- to develop concept knowledge

PURPOSE

- To enable students to comprehend and remember new information through organizing and recording in unique and creative ways.

OVERVIEW

Mind maps help students organize the content of a text that has been read, heard, or viewed. This is achieved by providing formats that assist in summarizing their thoughts and information, and provides a plan for writing or oral presentations.

Some mind maps are also referred to as concept maps.

MATERIALS

- A variety of writing materials
- The use of color adds emphasis

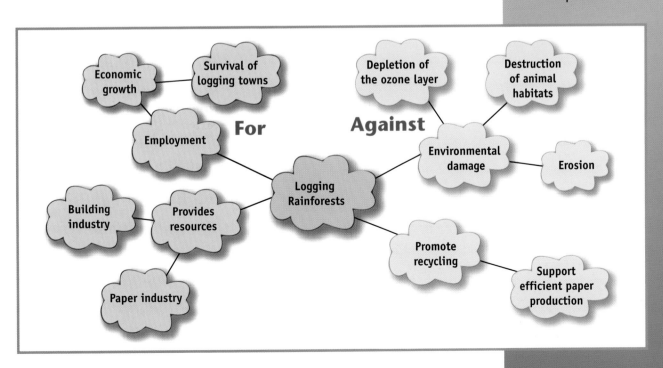

PURPOSE

- This procedure supports students in locating words that are displayed in the classroom environment.

OVERVIEW

The students can then use the words located as a reference during independent writing. Depending on the developmental level of the student writing, the print displayed around the room can be used as a stimulus for writing. This is still a valuable writing activity for older students.

MATERIALS

- A chart showing the stages of the writing process
- High frequency word wall
- Word family charts
- Phonogram charts
- Charts with examples of a variety of written genres
- Students' own published work, such as:
  - posters
  - murals
  - student-made books
  - lists of interest or topic words
  - name chart
  - boxes of spelling words
  - word of the week display board

PROCEDURE

1. Demonstrate to students that there are many ways they can access words when writing independently. This can be modeled to a whole class by using questioning techniques. For example:

   Where in our class would I look to find the correct spelling of the word *because*?

   Where in our class would I look to find a word that rhymes with *night*?

2. Students can then work in pairs, asking similar questions of each other.

3. After gathering a list of words from around the room, students could:

   - put each word in a sentence
   - use as many of the words as possible in one sentence
   - make a word web
   - put the words in alphabetical order
   - use dictionaries to find the correct meaning of the words

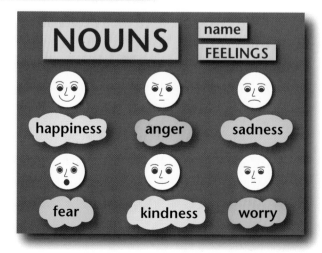

PROCEDURE

Independent writing center tasks will provide opportunities for students to engage in developing a wide range of texts in a variety of forms for real purposes. Writing tasks should be integrated into the context of existing classroom focuses.

Independent writing tasks can be established to provide opportunities for students to:

- extend existing knowledge and understandings
- investigate particular interests
- develop existing writing focuses
- develop particular linguistic skills and understandings
- develop conceptual knowledge about particular topics
- write for enjoyment to express ideas

Students will be required to draw on their knowledge of composing and shaping texts to complete tasks while considering the purpose and audience for the writing.

Independent writing includes collaborative writing by pairs or small groups of students, independent of the teacher.

Teachers need to ensure that they have provided opportunities for students to develop strategies related to text construction, including knowledge of:

- grammatical structures, features, and conventions of texts, including spelling, grammar, punctuation, and sentence structure
- text organization, including generic structures
- purposes and intended audiences
- layout and presentation options

Establish organizational procedures for students in order to:

- ensure ease of access to the variety of materials available for use during independent writing
- provide visual support materials as scaffolds for independent tasks
- store drafts or incomplete pieces of work for future retrieval
- undertake editing and proofreading practices independent of the teacher

Ensure that students are familiar with the expectations for independent writing tasks. For example, if they are developing an information report, they will be familiar with the generic structure of a report, will have been explicitly taught strategies for locating information from a variety of sources, will have an understanding of how to use this information to shape their writing, and be aware of a variety of layout and presentation practices that they can use to publish their report.

PURPOSE

- To promote writing as a rewarding, enjoyable, and creative activity.

OVERVIEW

Students are to write independently, using a wide variety of genres.
By participating in exciting and interesting writing centers, students will be motivated and see a purpose for their writing.

Opportunities to write should be both independent and cooperative.

MATERIALS

- A variety of writing materials and different types of paper
- A computer for publishing students' work
- Folded cards and small made-up blank books
- A utility box containing staplers, scissors, paperclips, rubber bands, sticky notes, tape, date stamp, and hole punches
- A selection of dictionaries
- A "Have a go" book, where students can try to spell a word before checking the correct spelling
- Plastic sheet protectors or folders in which to keep drafts of students' work
- A box containing stimulus pictures based on the interests of the class
- Writing support charts, such as *Who, What, When, Where, Why,* and *Feelings*
- Punctuation charts

Organizational considerations are crucial to the success of the computer center. Familiarity with the software and the ability to work collaboratively as part of a small group or independently is vital. Students need to have had ample opportunities to develop the necessary skills and understandings before they will be able to become actively engaged in computer center tasks. Before they are able to work independently or interdependently in the computer center, they should have been involved in discussions, modeled use, and active construction and deconstruction of a variety of text types.

Students need to have time to experiment with software in order to discover what options are available to them. As with all literacy center activities, the computer center must have a clearly defined purpose and a clear teacher expectation of learning outcomes.

Computer-based learning can be successfully integrated into many learning situations to enhance and extend student literacy and language learning. A wide variety of software programs can be used to implement a diverse range of teaching and learning ideas. Meaningful contexts for listening, reading, writing, and viewing can be created through the use of various types of software in the classroom.

Speaking and listening skills can be encouraged through the social context; that is, created when students are working with open-ended software such as paint and draw, word games, adventure games, and simulations.

Paint and draw and word programs create opportunities to draft, edit, format, save, and print texts. Illustrations and/or graphics can be added to support student-written texts. The flexibility of these programs enables students to be successful at their own ability level and promotes risk-taking, using the advantage of the "undo" option.

Adventure games and simulations involve a high degree of problem solving and decision making. Students using this software are required to theorize, justify, hypothesize, and explain. This also provides a context for listening, speaking, and writing across a wide range of curriculum areas. Simulations also enable students to experience aspects of the real world they would not normally be exposed to. They are motivated to enquire, research, and test hypotheses and then report the results of their findings. Publisher programs enable students to present their ideas in a variety of formats that reflect the purpose of the text and the intended audience. Using desktop publishing, students can create and publish texts with a high degree of flexibility in terms of layout,

▲
Preparing to move to the computer center

combinations of words and graphics, and a variety of fonts and text styles. With a clearly defined purpose, publisher programs can be highly motivating for all students, and the computer center is an essential option for all successful literacy-focused classrooms.

Electronic texts, such as "living books," multimedia resources, databases, and electronic bulletin boards, widen students' exposure to a range of text types that will be increasingly important to them in the future. Through the computer center, students are provided with opportunities to construct and deconstruct a wide variety of texts, just as they are able to do with printed texts.

"Living books" are often adaptations of well-known children's books. They are motivational and assist in engaging reluctant readers through the use of sound, appealing graphics, and animation. Teachers can then plan related activities that the students can engage in to demonstrate their understanding in much the same way that a printed text is used. Data software can contain information about a specific subject or allow the user to enter his or her own data. Using this type of software enables students to learn about the conventions of factual language in a way that is supportive and motivational. As previously stated, familiarization with the software is essential and contextualization of the topic is equally important. The above points need to be considered when setting up a computer center.

Working in the classroom computer center

Telecommunications software opens up students' writing to a wider and more diverse audience. The sending and receiving of e-mail, information retrieval, and exchange of ideas and resources are common uses for this form of software. Through accessing the Internet, students are able to communicate over distances, discuss issues, and exchange ideas. When researching topics, they are required to make decisions about the relevance of the information collected and which parts of this to download to meet their purposes. For example, students need to ask who the audience will be and therefore question the relevance of the information. This could be downloaded for class books, newsletters, posters, and projects. In order to do this, students require prior experience in integrating the use of word processing and publishing software so that they can work independently.

Computer centers can be highly motivating for all students and provide a wide range of opportunities for them to extend and consolidate their literacy skills. These centers also provide opportunities for students to engage with and complete motivational tasks in collaboration with others. The work completed gives teachers an excellent means of assessing the many literacy skills students will need to master through the use of this center.

PURPOSE

- To provide students with the opportunities to identify the difference between fact and opinion from information found through using the Internet.

OVERVIEW

Use the current interests of students to research information available on the Internet. Students then discuss and justify whether the information collected is fact or opinion.

MATERIALS

- Computer with access to the Internet
- Highlighter pens of various colors

PROCEDURE

Work individually, in pairs, or in small groups.

1. Select a variety of information on a particular topic and print it out.

2. Read and discuss it.

3. Identify statements of fact, highlighting them in one color, and statements of opinion, highlighting them in another color.

4. Repeat this with all the collected information.

5. Share responses with the whole class. Students are also to justify why they decided to label the piece of information chosen as fact or opinion.

In the example below, information was collected from the Internet and color-coded to distinguish fact from opinion.

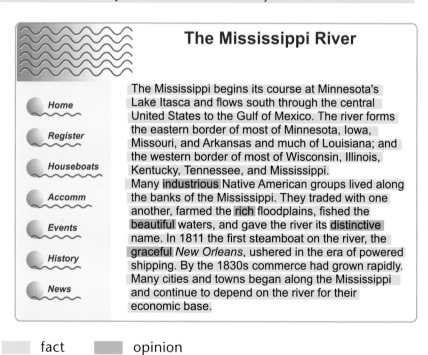

PROCEDURE

1. Teacher prepares a message containing misspelled words.

   This message could:

   - be a sample of the students' own writing

   - relate to a familiar text

   - focus on a particular grammatical feature

   - reinforce a generic structure

2. Students:

   - locate errors, delete, and correct

   - activate the spellcheck to correct misspellings

   - choose between several spellings

   See the following example.

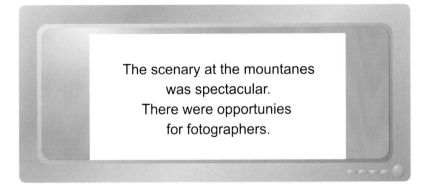

The scenary at the mountanes
was spectacular.
There were opportunies
for fotographers.

3. Print the message for checking. By not saving the changes, the message can be reused.

Proofreading on screen

PURPOSE

- To focus students' attention on the importance of spelling as a functional aspect of writing.

OVERVIEW

Students are provided with opportunities to practice editing and proofreading text without the distraction of the mechanics of writing. The teacher is then able to help students develop specific spelling and knowledge about the writing, for example: visual knowledge, morphemic knowledge, and etymological knowledge.

MATERIALS

- Teacher-prepared message accessed by computer

PURPOSE

- To give students the skills to analyze, sort, and use information gained through computer-mediated sources.

OVERVIEW

Students will develop the skills to set purposes, question self and peers, apply information, and comprehend.

There will also be opportunities for using word processing and publishing software. This involves composing, editing, publishing, and presenting.

MATERIALS

- Access to information that is related to a class topic. Students could use newspapers or the Internet to research a current issue or event.

PROCEDURE

Teachers should explain the purpose for collecting the information with the end product clearly stated, for example, a report, a project, or a presentation to the class.

The student or students work through six steps while accessing information:

1. *Deciding* – What is it that I/we really want to find out? (This should be done prior to accessing a website.)

2. *Finding* – Where can I find the information I need? What do I already know? (This should also take place prior to using the technology.)

3. *Using* – Which parts of the information found do I really need to use? (printout)

4. *Recording* – How can I best use this information?

5. *Presenting* – How will I/we present this information?

6. *Evaluation* – Did I/we achieve what I/we set out to do? What were some of the important things I/we learned from this?

The above steps can be modeled by the teacher and then displayed on a chart in the computer center as a student guide for researching information.

1. Have you decided what it is you want to find out more about?

2. Where will you look for the information you need?

3. Which parts of the information do you need, and which parts do you not need?

4. How can you best use this information?

5. How will you present your information?

6. Did you achieve what you set out to achieve? What have you learned?

PROCEDURE

Students are organized into small groups of three or four, with one student as the leader. In the photograph below, Jane has selected the title card "Tropical Rainforests" from the class box of known book titles. The members of the group sit in a circle and ask questions, attempting to guess the title. Jane can only answer "yes" or "no" to the questions. Some of the questions asked by this group were:

Is the book fiction?

Is the book nonfiction?

Are there animals in the book?

Is the book about growing things?

Are there photographs in the book?

Is the author a man?

As the leader, Jane keeps a tally of how many questions are asked. After fifteen questions, Katerina guesses the correct title. It is then her turn to choose a title from the box.

ASPECTS OF TEXT

- characters
- author (male or female?)
- fiction/nonfiction
- illustrations
- photographs
- chapters
- colorful
- amusing
- happy/sad ending
- interesting facts
- animals

PURPOSE

- To encourage students to recall and discuss texts they have read.

OVERVIEW

Students are provided with a set procedure for questioning the person who has chosen one text from titles written on cards. The aim is for the group to guess the title by looking at the poster that displays aspects of a text, and using it to form questions.

MATERIALS

- A set of cards, each showing one title of a book that the majority of the students have read

- A poster displaying aspects of texts that will support the group in forming the questions to be asked

▲
Preparing to answer questions about the book *Tropical Rainforests*

CHANGING TEXT FORM

PURPOSE

- Students demonstrate their comprehension of a text through their representation of it in a different form.

OVERVIEW

By changing the text into another format, students are required to use higher order thinking skills to identify main ideas. It is important for the students to understand that the meaning of the text must be maintained.

MATERIALS

Materials required will vary, depending on the form chosen. Some essential materials are:

- Selection of clothing and material for drama activities

- Blank format of a comic strip

- Selection of art materials – pens, crayons, paints, pencils, and collage paper for visual representation of a text

PROCEDURE

Students work individually, in pairs, or in small groups, to change the form of the original text. Forms may include:

- dramatization

- comic strip

- story map

- picture book

- journal

- story board

- visual interpretation

- song

The examples below are from *Daniel and the Doors,* written by Nette Hilton and published by Longman.

PROCEDURE

Discuss with students the purpose of keeping a diary and the genre of diary writing. Ensure that students understand that entries are written in the first person and the importance of dating all entries.

Once taught, the character diary provides a novel alternative for students to respond to texts they are reading.

The character diary assists students who may have difficulty in sequencing a "snapshot." A cognitive organizer of events can be used prior to the diary writing.

The following example of a character diary is adapted from *Uncle Ben's Fishing Trip*, written by Gretchen Brassington and published by Dominie Press.

In this example, the writer has chosen to be Cassie, one of the main characters in the book, and record the story through her diary entries.

Friday, June 3

Dear Diary,

It's been a long time since I've seen my cousin Kevin. We used to live along the same country road, and we spent a lot of time playing together. Then two years ago my parents and I moved to Hawaii. We're back now, and my dad says Kevin is going fishing with us tomorrow. I'm really looking forward to seeing him.

Saturday, June 4

Dear Diary,

We had a great day on the boat. We saw a huge whale, and I had a chance to move into the helm seat and pilot the Sea Flight. *And to top it all off, Kevin caught a great-looking fish! But he seemed different somehow. He used to be adventurous and full of life. But on the boat, he seemed afraid and so quiet. And when he caught that big fish, he looked like he was going to be sick! Before we went back ashore, Kevin and I had a chance to talk.*

Sunday, June 5

Dear Diary,

I'm glad I talked with Kevin yesterday. I told him that I think he's sensitive and that he loves animals. He thought he was just being squeamish. After being apart for two years, I guess we both noticed changes in each other. But I think we're going to be good friends again, now that my parents and I are back.

PURPOSE

- To encourage students to respond to a text, using the genre of diary writing. This activity also encourages students to practice the skill of sequencing events in chronological order.

OVERVIEW

During the reading of a chapter book, students take on the role of one of the main characters and make diary entries about events and the feelings and emotions of the character.

MATERIALS

- Examples of diaries or entries from diaries

- Genre sheet showing the construction and layout of a diary entry

- Photocopied formats of diary pages that students can then compile into their own character diaries

CHARACTER WEB

PURPOSE

- To provide opportunities to interpret and evaluate information at literal, inferential, and critical levels to build a "picture" of a chosen character.

OVERVIEW

This literacy challenge assists students to see relationships between different characters and situations and to make personal judgments about these.

Students are also involved in making inferences about characters and the part they play in the story (reading between the lines).

Students are also asked to put themselves in the character's situation and to consider each character's point of view (critical reading beyond the text).

MATERIALS

- A familiar narrative text, biography, autobiography, or factual text containing characters

- Writing materials

PROCEDURE

Students work independently, in pairs, or in small groups.

1. Using a familiar text, students self-select a character to be analyzed. Alternatively the character may be predetermined by the teacher.

2. Place the character's name in the center of the page.

3. Brainstorm characteristics. Consider personal actions and interactions with other characters. Consider literal, implied, and inferred information in order to justify interpretations and judgments.

4. Organize the brainstormed information around the central title to build up a complete "picture" of the character. Subheadings may be useful.

5. Consider what style of lines to use, use of color, pictures, and symbols to emphasize points and create a feel for the character.

6. Share the character web with others during sharing time, justifying opinions. Discuss alternative points of view if they arise.

7. Display the character webs in the classroom.

The following is an example of a character web from *Daniel and the Doors,* written by Nette Hilton and published by Longman.

In this example the student has chosen to show different aspects of the character:

- the kind of person the character is
- the problems he had
- the solutions that were tried
- other characters who helped
- the best thing the character achieved or did in the story

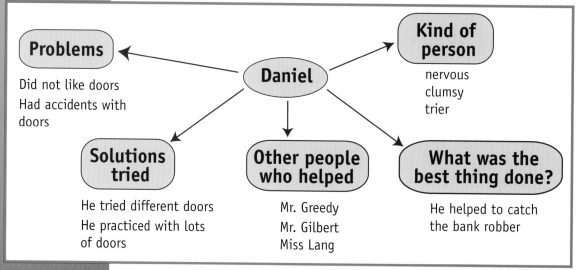

PROCEDURE

This strategy is best introduced and practiced as a whole class. It can then be used by individuals or small groups of students working together in a literacy center.

1. Display the picture where all the students can easily see it and discuss where it has come from and why you have chosen this particular picture.

2. Show the group an example of a sensory wheel (see example on the next page). Explain that you are going to have the students work in small groups. Each group will be given a section of the wheel and will be responsible for making some responses about their particular section.

3. Divide the class into five groups.

4. Appoint a scribe for each group and remind the groups that all ideas are acceptable and everyone in the group must have an equal say.

5. Cut the wheel into five sections, giving one section to each group.

6. Explain to the groups that they have to imagine they are standing somewhere in this picture.

7. Using the picture, the students brainstorm and record all the things that they can see, hear, feel, smell, or taste, depending on which section of the wheel their group is given to work on.

8. Allow about twenty minutes for the group discussion and to allow time for the students to absorb the many details in the picture.

9. When the recording is complete, ask a representative from each group to bring out their section of the wheel and share a few examples with the class.

10. As this is done, the sensory wheel can be put back together to provide an excellent ongoing resource for:

    - poetry or song writing

    - creative story writing

    - oral discussion on a topic

    - word study (grouping of similar words either by meaning or word families)

EXAMPLE OF A SENSORY WHEEL

The example on the next page comes from *The Otherwhere Ice Show*, written by Gail Kimberly, illustrated by Mario Capaldi, and published by Dominie Press. Photocopy Page 12 of the book and place it on an overhead transparency. If sufficient copies of the book are available, the text can be used.

PURPOSE

- To provide students with an excellent strategy that can be used to respond to any visual text.

OVERVIEW

Students respond to a visual text, using a circle divided into five sections. This encourages them to focus on details that relate to each of the five senses.

MATERIALS

- Either a large, interesting picture with lots of detail or a similar picture that has been copied onto an overhead transparency

Explain to the class that you are going to ask the students to put themselves in this picture, and that in a small group they will brainstorm what they would be able to see, hear, touch, smell, and taste, using as many descriptive words as possible. A large circle is then cut into six sections, five representing the senses, and one labeled "Feelings." The students brainstorm on this piece of paper. Appoint one student as the scribe and allow approximately ten minutes for ideas to be discussed and observations to be made, with an additional ten minutes for responses to be recorded.

Each group then reads their responses aloud, and the wheel is put back together again. The example below shows the detail and descriptive language that this process encourages.

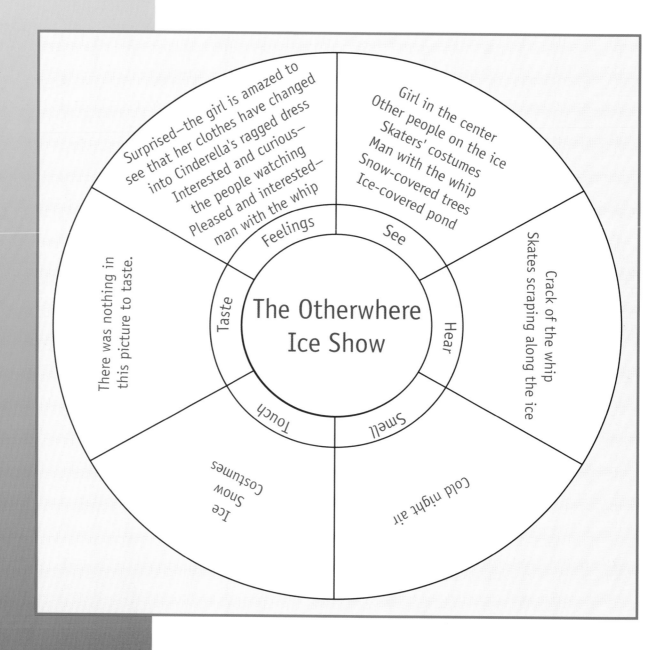

PROCEDURE

Introduce and practice this strategy initially with the whole class. When students become confident with this process, a leader can be appointed to a small group. Using a picture from a read text, this student can lead the rest of the group through the visualization process.

EXAMPLE OF A TEACHER-LED VISUALIZATION PROCESS WITH THE WHOLE CLASS:

> Make sure you are all sitting comfortably, with nothing in your hands. Close your eyes. I am going to ask you to make some pictures inside your head.
>
> I want you to make a picture of a large bowl of ice cream. Decide what color the ice cream is. Is there one scoop or lots of scoops? Have a look at the dish the ice cream is in. Make the dish a very special dish. Look at the color you have made the dish. On top of the ice cream put something very special and different. Make a picture of a spoon next to your dish of ice cream. What does this spoon look like? In your head, pick up this spoon and take a large scoop of ice cream. Put it into your mouth and taste the flavor. When I count to five I want you to open your eyes and share your ice cream picture with a partner. One … two … three … four … five …

The students then share the pictures they have made. This oral sharing can be followed by artwork or writing.

The visualization process can be used very successfully to encourage students to respond to a text. The following example uses *Wildlife in the City*, written by Jean Bennett and published by Dominie Press. A teacher or student leader could use this process to visualize the lizard discussed in the book. The students could then visualize the lizard — how it felt and how it smelled.

> Imagine that you saw a lizard like the one featured in *Wildlife in the City*. Make a picture inside your head of what the lizard looks like. What color are you going to make it? How big is the lizard? Now pretend you picked up the lizard and put it in a box. Is it heavy? Is it trying to move? Think about what it feels like. Is it soft or hard? Is it rough or smooth? Does it feel slippery? Does it feel slimy? Is it wet? Inside your head, put your nose near the lizard and smell it. What does it smell like? Now you are going to take the lizard to school. See yourself walking into school with the lizard placed carefully in a box. Make a picture of you sitting in class with the lizard on your desk. What are you going to do with the lizard? When I count to five, open your eyes and share your pictures with a partner. One … two … three … four … five …

PURPOSE

- To provide students with a simple structure that enhances responses to any text in a creative manner.

OVERVIEW

Students learn to use visualization techniques to think about what they have read.

MATERIALS

- Because this is a process, the only material required is a text that has been read by the whole class or the small group of students working at this center.

PURPOSE

- To encourage students to respond to a text in which the author is expressing how things are alike or different.

OVERVIEW

Students will learn to recognize and use cue words such as *different*, *in contrast*, *same as*, *or*, *on the other hand*.

Students will also experience the benefit of using a graphic organizer to support their responses to the text.

MATERIALS

- Several large laminated cards with the outline of a Venn diagram on each card

- Wet erase pens

- Multiple copies of an article or a chapter from a book

PROCEDURE

This can be done as an individual or group activity. However, as with most of the activities in this book, group discussion assists with clarification and justification of ideas and statements.

1. Students read the text and through discussion complete the Venn diagram.

2. This graphic organizer can then be used as an outline for a piece of writing, highlighting, comparing, and contrasting a text.

The following example of a Venn diagram is based on *Arctic Foxes and Red Foxes*, written by Graham Meadows and Claire Vial, and published by Dominie Press.

Arctic Foxes

They live around the Arctic Circle. They weigh between six and fifteen pounds and have very thick fur to keep them warm. They eat lemmings and small animals like rodents, squirrels, hares, seal pups, and birds.

Both

have excellent vision and hearing.

Red Foxes

They live in warmer regions of North America, Europe, Asia, and North Africa. They are about twice as big as Arctic foxes. They eat plants, berries, beetles, and earthworms. They also catch and eat small prey.

◀ **Reading the text before a discussion period**

PROCEDURE

1. Five or six students choose or are given a role card. The teacher ensures that the students are clear as to what aspect of the text they are focusing on.

2. The students then read the text to themselves, making notes as they go.

3. The group waits until each member has finished reading.

4. They then share their responses, one at a time.

ROLES

1. **Predictor** – This role does not require any note-taking until the reading is completed. The student then writes down his or her predictions about what will happen next, in terms of events, character behavior, etc.

2. **Event recorder** – During the reading, this student records the main events that occur.

3. **Setting recorder** – This role involves taking notes during the reading about the different settings in the text and then describing them.

4. **Character reporter** – This role involves recording aspects of each of the characters in the text.

5. **Problem/solution recorder** – This student records any problems that occur and any solutions.

6. **Quote recorder** – The role of this student is to record any important quotes that the main characters may have said.

7. **Word finder** – The role of this student is to record any difficult or interesting words in the text and to look up their meanings in a dictionary.

8. **Summarizer** – This student summarizes the chapter or article in a few sentences.

PURPOSE

- To heighten the comprehension skills of students through sharing different aspects of a text.

OVERVIEW

Each student is given a different role to carry out during the reading of a book chapter or a short article.

MATERIALS

- A variety of cards with a role written on each one

- Multiple copies of a book or an article

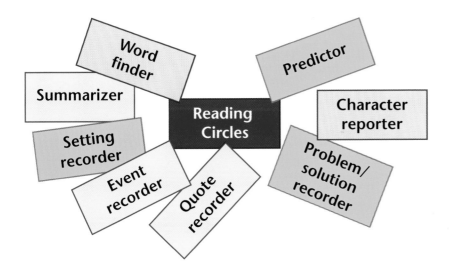

EXAMPLE:

The following example is based on *Lookout Boy*, written by Elizabeth Van Steenwyk, and published by Dominie Press.

These are possible responses from a group of fourth grade students after reading *Lookout Boy*.

EVENT RECORDER

David wanted to be a lookout boy, watching for ships that bring supplies to the city.

Uncle Zeb said that David was too little, and that the other boys would play tricks on him, but David would not give up.

Silas and the other older boys teased David and took his lunch pail. David felt sad because he wanted to make friends with the other boys.

The first ship David spotted turned out to be a ship full of garbage. But when he saved the town by spotting an approaching fire, the older boys decided he was a great lookout boy.

CHARACTER REPORTER

David – Wanted to be a lookout boy.

Uncle Zeb – Wasn't sure David was old enough to be his lookout boy.

Silas – Took David's lunch pail and teased him.

Joe and John – Joined Silas in teasing David.

QUOTE RECORDER

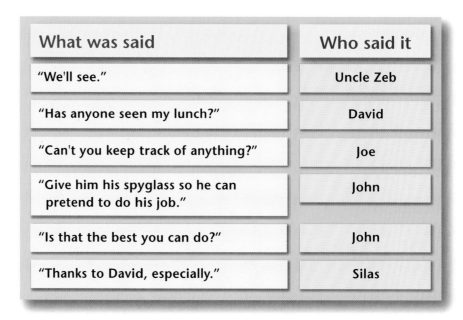

What was said	Who said it
"We'll see."	Uncle Zeb
"Has anyone seen my lunch?"	David
"Can't you keep track of anything?"	Joe
"Give him his spyglass so he can pretend to do his job."	John
"Is that the best you can do?"	John
"Thanks to David, especially."	Silas

PREDICTOR

I think that, after David saved the town, he and the older boys would become good friends, and that David would continue to be a lookout boy for his Uncle Zeb.

PROBLEM/SOLUTION RECORDER

The Problem	Who the Problem Belonged To	The Solution
David wanted to be a lookout boy.	David	He asked Uncle Zeb for the job.
The older boys kept taking David's lunch pail.	David	He played a trick on them.
It was very hot on the lookout hill.	The lookout boys	The older boys rested in the shade.
The other boys didn't think David was ready to be a lookout boy.	David and the other boys (because they didn't give him a chance)	David saved the town by spotting a fire.

Looking for a solution ➤ to a problem

PURPOSE

- To encourage students to reflect critically on what they have read, using higher levels of comprehension skills.

OVERVIEW

During or after the reading of a book, students make comments or predictions about the text they have read.

MATERIALS

- A small exercise journal for each student

- Examples of formats that can be chosen by students when responding to a text

PROCEDURE

Students should be encouraged to write in their journals several times a week.

1. Model for students, showing how to give specific examples and thoughtful explanations that support their responses.

2. Journals should not be overused and become a chore that students don't wish to undertake. Journals are a way in which students can connect what they have read to real life and their own experiences.

3. Students can choose to respond to a completed book or to make journal entries after reading several chapters.

4. Many teachers encourage the use of journals during independent reading time.

5. All journal entries should be dated, with the title and author of the book clearly shown at the beginning of each entry.

Following are some formats that can be made available for students. However, students should also have the choice to design their own response formats, or to simply freewrite about their books.

Date_____   Name_____

Title_____

Author_____

CHARACTERS	SETTING	EVENTS

CHARACTERS	QUOTES

PHRASES I COULD USE IN MY WRITING	PROBLEMS	HOW PROBLEMS WERE SOLVED

Date_____   Name_____

Title_____

Author_____

THIS IS HOW THE BOOK/ CHAPTER ENDED	THIS IS HOW I WOULD CHANGE IT

IF I WERE A CHARACTER IN THE BOOK I WOULD BE...	THINGS I WOULD DO OR SAY THE SAME AS IN THE BOOK	THINGS I WOULD DO OR SAY DIFFERENTLY THAN IN THE BOOK

Date: 10/20/03

Title: Daniel and the Doors

Author: Nette Hilton

Illustrator: Martin Bailey

Characters	Setting	Plot
Daniel	In the supermarket	Daniel couldn't open doors.
Miss Lang	Mr. Gilbert's shop	He tried lots
The Robber	the post office	of doors
Mr. Fuzby	The bank	On a class
Mr. Gilbert		trip he got stuck in the bank door and caught a bank robber

Date: 10/24/03
Title: Daniel and the Doors
Author: Nette Hilton
Illustrator: Martin Bailey

If I were Daniel I would have got somebody to teach me about doors. I would have felt brave too if I caught a robber. I would ask if I could have a reward for catching the robber.

ANALYZING NEWSPAPER PHOTOGRAPHS

PURPOSE

- To help students consolidate their understanding of photos as constructions.

- To analyze and interpret meaning from newspaper photos.

- To draw conclusions about the intent of the photos.

OVERVIEW

Students will have prior experience in considering how their own experiences, culture, and context as viewers influence their interpretations of photographs.

They will draw on prior knowledge and understanding of photographic techniques that can influence interpretations (size, camera angle, position, direction, body language, clothing, and focus).

This literacy activity will consolidate students' understanding of issues related to gender, stereotypes, emotional intent, impact on the reader, and intended and unintended messages.

MATERIALS

- Newspaper photos (Laminate all of these for durability.)

- Accompanying headings

- Additional information about how, when, why and where the photos were taken (optional)

- Photos used could have a specific focus, e.g., sports photos, newspaper front page, political, travel, and so on.

PROCEDURE

Modeled and shared experiences in critical analysis of photos is required prior to students being expected to complete this activity in a literacy center situation. Critical analysis by a small group provides opportunities for students to develop skills in working cooperatively.

SINGLE PHOTO ANALYSIS

1. Initially students analyze the photo according to criteria determined by the teacher, i.e., a set of focus questions.

2. Students discuss the questions and record their responses.

3. Students decide on an appropriate heading for the photo. This could then be compared with the heading that accompanies the photo. This would provide opportunities for further discussion.

4. Additional information about when, why, and how the photo was taken could then be read. Students reassess their interpretations, given the additional information.

5. Students report to the whole group during sharing time.

6. As students become more familiar with the critical analysis of photos, self-selected criteria for analysis may be expected.

7. If the students are analyzing a set of photos, they will be required to make generalizations with regard to the intent, photographic techniques used, impact on the audience, and so on.

Students analyzing newspaper photographs

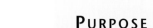

PROCEDURE

1. In pairs or small groups, students discuss their opinions of the chosen character. A chart such as the one below can be used initially to support discussion.

2. Students then decide on ways they might represent their character – this can be through words, diagrams, overhead transparencies, or dramatization.

3. Illustrations can be used to support points made by the students.

4. Completed points of view can be shared at whole-class sharing time, with all students either agreeing or disagreeing with the presenter by a show of hands.

   In an excellent extension of this activity, the students write about the character from the viewpoint of one of the other characters from the same source.

PURPOSE

- To develop an understanding of characters that students have read about, heard about, or viewed. Students then form and justify their views of the chosen character.

OVERVIEW

The teacher or a small group of students choose a character from a known source. Students then discuss and justify their opinions about the character. Following this, students create a representation of the character.

MATERIALS

- Materials will vary according to the form of character representation chosen by the teacher or the students.

CHARACTER POINT OF VIEW

Do you think the character is:

- Good/bad?
- Beautiful/ugly?
- Kind/selfish?
- Sensible/silly?
- Well-mannered/rude?
- Funny/serious?
- Angry/calm?
- Happy/sad?
- Clever/stupid?

Maggie is the ▶ main character of *The Otherwhere Ice Show*. These students will share their points of view about Maggie when they have finished reading the book.

RESPONDING CRITICALLY TO ADVERTISEMENTS

PURPOSE

- To encourage students to extend their critical literacy skills through the genre of an advertisement.

OVERVIEW

Students critically analyze advertisements, identifying values, attitudes, and cultural messages that may be intended or unintended in texts. This will help them to recognize how texts can influence readers and viewers, and allow them to understand that the main idea or intention of a text can be open to interpretation.

It will also provide opportunities for students to "interrogate" advertisements, encouraging them to comprehend, monitor, evaluate, and reaffirm their understandings of texts.

MATERIALS

- A selection of newspaper, magazine, or television advertisements to be read or viewed

- The advertisements may focus on a particular theme, e.g., Valentine's Day or Father's Day.

PROCEDURE

Prior experience in critically analyzing advertisements is necessary before introducing this literacy center.

Analyzing texts in pairs or small groups enables students to engage in constructive conversations and requires them to develop skills appropriate to working cooperatively. The value of working together also provides opportunity for different interpretations to be identified and discussed.

1. Organize advertisements into individual texts to be analyzed, or these can grouped for viewing according to a common theme (for comparison).

   - Fast food
   - Beauty products
   - Travel
   - Electrical goods

2. Students may self-select the advertisement/s to be analyzed, or the ads may be predetermined by the teacher.

3. Students brainstorm the content, purpose, audience, and form of the advertisement and record their observations. A questioning guide or structured overview could be developed by the teacher to focus these observations.

4. Discuss and record the motivational techniques used, e.g., use of famous people, placement of objects, settings, use of music, lighting, jingles, slogans, and so on.

5. Identify social and cultural messages hidden in the text.

6. Share observations with the class during sharing time.

EXTENSION

(This may take several days to complete.)

1. As a group, design an advertisement for television or printed media.

2. For television, prepare a storyboard considering a variety of camera shots, logical sequence, information and graphics, format, product, audience, style of advertisement, use of color, and so on.

3. For printed media, consider the aspects noted in Step 2, in addition to layout, and present them in poster form.

4. Present the poster to the class in sharing time, explaining decisions made in creating the advertisement.

5. The teacher prepares criteria for assessment of advertisements presented, focusing on eye-catching presentation, persuasive language, and originality.

PROCEDURE

Prior experience in the development of sociograms is required before students can work independently.

1. Students can work independently or collaboratively in pairs or small groups to create a sociogram.

   There is a diversity of ways to construct sociograms, e.g., cut and paste, pen and paper, computer-generated, etc.

   The complexity of the text will affect the way the sociogram is constructed, as will the focus for critical analysis of the relationships.

2. Students individualize their representations by choosing a variety of arrow styles, character labels, symbols, colors, and so on.

   The following conventions may assist in creating sociograms:

   - Represent significant character/s centrally on the page.

   - Place other characters around the central character/s. The distance between characters could be representative of the "closeness" or "distance" of relationships between them.

   - Show the direction of a relationship, using an arrow accompanied by a brief but explicit label.

   - Substantiated or inferred relationships may be defined with the use of varied line styles or colors.

   - The use of pictures or symbols may assist representation of relationships.

   The example below comes from the text *Bull Harris and the Purple Ooze*, written by Julie Mitchell, and published by Longman. It shows the relationships between the group of children in the story.

3. Students share their sociograms with the class, explaining their interpretations of character relationships.

4. Evaluating sociograms and explanations provides insight for teachers into students' comprehension and their ability to critically analyze relationships in texts.

PURPOSE

- To critically analyze relationships between characters from a text that is read, heard, or viewed.

- To represent character relationships in the form of a graphic organizer.

- To provide an opportunity for students to explore literal and implied relationships.

OVERVIEW

The students or the teacher choose a text that contains a number of characters. Students identify and represent, in diagrammatical format, the relationships between the identified characters.

MATERIALS

- A variety of writing materials

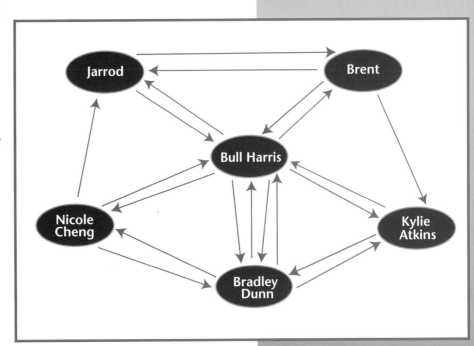

STRUCTURED CONTROVERSY

PURPOSE

- To encourage students to work collaboratively and to reach group consensus about a text that has been read, heard, or viewed.

OVERVIEW

A small group of students take turns at looking at different sides of a statement or opinion.

MATERIALS

- Cards with the two statements or opinions written on them

For example:

It should be made a law that students come to school on Saturdays, as well as the other five days.	*It would be a bad idea if students were made to come to school on Saturdays.*

Or:

In the story The Three Little Pigs, *the wolf had no right to threaten the pigs and eat two of them.*	*In the story* The Three Little Pigs, *the wolf had every right to try to eat the pigs if he was hungry.*

PROCEDURE

1. Either as a pair or as a small group, the students decide which side of the statement or opinion they are going to take.

2. They then spend five or ten minutes making notes about what they are going to say and the points they are going to make.

3. Each person or group then shares his or her responses. The others listen and then share the opposing responses.

4. The pair or groups then exchange the position they have just taken and again spend a few minutes making notes about what they are going to say.

5. It is important to stress that, after they have exchanged positions, they do not simply repeat what the first group said. They have to think of new reasons to back up their statements or opinions.

6. At the planning stage, students can use a diagram to show the different arguments put forward.

EXAMPLE

WE SHOULD GO TO SCHOOL ON SATURDAYS	IT WOULD NOT BE GOOD TO GO TO SCHOOL ON SATURDAYS
We would learn more things.	We would miss out on sports.
Other school days could end at lunchtime.	Everybody would get tired.
Parents who work on Saturdays would not have to find baby-sitters.	We would miss Saturday morning TV.
We could get longer holidays in exchange for all the Saturdays.	Our parents would not spend time with us.
	You couldn't go away for a weekend.

PROCEDURE

It is expected that the text has been read, heard, or viewed by students.

1. Working in pairs, the students identify the major points of the text.

2. They record these to share with others.

3. They may refer to the text.

4. Have each pair explain their decisions to others in the group.

5. As a group, discuss and demonstrate how and why their key points differed.

6. Display each pair's lists.

PURPOSE

- To encourage students to read for the purpose of identifying the main ideas and points in a written text.

OVERVIEW

Students demonstrate their comprehension of a text by identifying what they consider the key points. Students reflect on the main idea or ideas presented, major concepts, and generalizations in the text. This text may have been read, heard, or viewed.

Students demonstrate their ability to comprehend texts at literal, inferential, and evaluative levels.

MATERIALS

- Writing materials, e.g., pen and paper, overhead transparency and pens, individual cards marked one to ten (or any chosen number)

- A copy of the text (optional)

▲
Students work together ▷
to decide the ten
key points of the text
they have read

PURPOSE

- To help students develop the ability to define and write a report on the attributes of a character.

OVERVIEW

Students extend their comprehension skills through focusing on one of the characters from a recently read text. They then interpret, evaluate, and justify opinions through oral discussion before moving into written reporting.

MATERIALS

- Materials will vary, depending on whether this is an individual or a group activity. If students are working on a group character report, large sheets of paper and markers will be needed.

PROCEDURE

Students should be familiar with the genre of a report.

1. Either group or class discussion should take place prior to written character reports to model different viewpoints and justify opinions.

2. Cognitive organizers are a useful visual tool to assist with sorting and classifying aspects of a character, either before or after the written report. The following example of a character report is based on *Bull Harris and the Purple Ooze,* by Julie Mitchell, published by Longman.

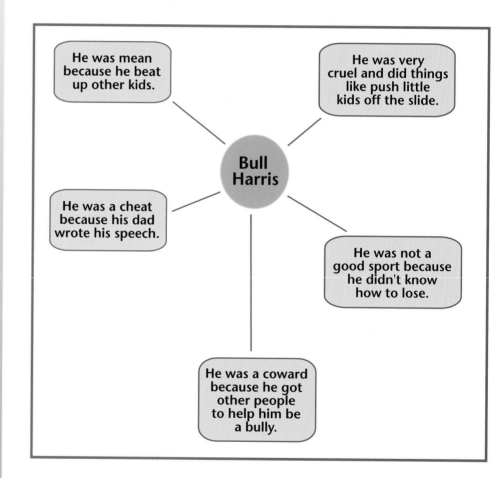

EXTENSION

Students who may have different viewpoints about a character in their written reports could debate and justify the content of their writing.

PROCEDURE

1. One student chooses a text card from the box and reads it aloud to the group.

2. Each member of the group takes it in turns to first decide if the text is fiction or nonfiction.

3. The group then discusses and justifies which label would best describe the text form.

4. The label is then placed next to the example and can be checked by the teacher when the activity is completed.

NONFICTION

In most ant species, workers go out to search for food on their own. When a worker finds a new food source, it returns to the colony, laying a scent trail. This trail leads other workers to the food. They follow the scent, forming a column. Then they collect the food and bring it back to nest.

AN EXPLANATION
Describes the characteristics and features of a particular thing.

Example from *Ants*, written by Graham Meadows and Claire Vial, and published by Dominie Press.

FICTION

Maggie glided around the pool and built up speed. Her heart jumped into her throat. She could feel it beating harder as she got ready for the jump. Then, almost without trying, she leaped into two perfect turns and landed gracefully.

A NARRATIVE
Tells a story. Has characters, settings, and plot.

Example from *The Otherwhere Ice Show*, written by Gail Kimberly and published by Dominie Press.

NONFICTION

Last week our class went to the lake for our school camp. We took our sleeping bags and we stayed in cabins. When we went down to the lake, Peter fell in with all his clothes on. It was very funny. When we went walking in the forest, we saw some squirrels and a green snake.

A RECOUNT
Retelling or recounting of past events.

Example from a fifth grade student writing after a school field trip.

PURPOSE

- To assist students with their understanding of the structure and features of a variety of text forms.

OVERVIEW

Students discuss a variety of photocopied text forms and then label each form appropriately, justifying their choices.

MATERIALS

- Text form labels
- A box containing cards showing different examples of text forms, such as:
  – a letter
  – a recipe
  – a narrative
  – a description
  – a recount
  – a report
  – an explanation
  – an invitation
  – a persuasive text, such as an advertisement

PURPOSE

- To consolidate understanding of the organizational structure of a report. (This can be adapted to any genre structure.)

OVERVIEW

Students reconstruct a report and name the components of this genre.

MATERIALS

- Examples of written reports, cut into clusters of information
- Cards with headings relating to the information contained in the text

PROCEDURE

- Read the puzzle pieces and discuss the information contained in each piece.
- Decide which heading best summarizes the information.
- Match the information to the organizational headings.
- The students' own written reports could be used to make the "puzzle" pieces for others.
- This procedure could be followed to consolidate understanding of the organizational structure of any genre that the students have been exposed to.

Title: (name of animal)	**Lizards**
Classification: (What family they belong to)	Lizards belong to the reptile family. They have scaly skin and are cold-blooded.
Description: (What they look like)	Most lizards have eyelids and ears. Some lizards can grow as long as a car. The smallest lizards only grow as long as a little finger.
Place/Time: (Where they live)	Lizards live in sunny places. Some live in the ground, and others live in trees and shrubs.
Dynamics: (What they do)	Some female lizards lay eggs. Other female lizards give birth to live babies.
Summarizing Comment: (An interesting fact)	Some lizards can change color.

PROCEDURE

Students need to be exposed to aspects of storytelling, such as:

- what makes a good story
- story selection
- interests of the audience
- roles in the storytelling session
- any props, such as puppets, that could be added to the session.

1. As a group, students choose a title of a well-known story.

2. Through discussion, students adapt the story line to fit the intended audience. (It is often a confidence boost to initially have students prepare a storytelling session for younger students.)

3. Students need to address two main issues: a) the suitability of the story; and b) the way the story should be told.

4. Students need time to practice their story, thinking about emphasis on words, facial expression, and making eye contact with the audience. These aspects could be displayed on a chart for the students to follow.

5. The storytelling session can be an individual telling to a group, a shared storytelling involving a group of students, or a videotaped storytelling session.

PURPOSE

- To develop oral language skills through shared storytelling.

- To encourage students to adapt a known text for a specific audience.

OVERVIEW

Students will become familiar and confident with aspects of storytelling.

MATERIALS

- Cards with titles of well-known stories

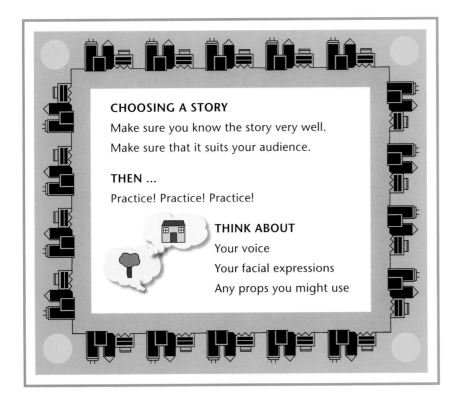

CHOOSING A STORY

Make sure you know the story very well.

Make sure that it suits your audience.

THEN ...

Practice! Practice! Practice!

THINK ABOUT

Your voice

Your facial expressions

Any props you might use

TEXT RECONSTRUCTION

PURPOSE

- To enable students to recognize the elements that make up a variety of genres.

OVERVIEW

Using samples of three or four familiar genres, the students recreate the correct components under each genre heading.

MATERIALS

- Cards with the components of genres written on them

- Heading cards with the name of the genre written on them

PROCEDURE

1. The students first locate the heading cards with the name of the genre and set these out.

2. Through discussion they decide which of the component cards go with each of the genres. Students must justify their choices. For example, a student placing a purpose card under the procedural genre heading would say:

   This card must go under the procedural heading because it states that the purpose is to show how something is accomplished through a series of steps.

3. During this activity, the discussion between students assists in clearly identifying the differences between certain genres. This process will transfer learning skills to their writing. This activity can be checked with genre charts, which should be available in all classrooms.

Procedural genre	Report genre	Explanation genre
To show how something is accomplished	To present factual information about a certain group and describe its characteristics	To explain how things are and why they are, or how things work
Opening statement, goal, or aim	Opening definition or classification	A general statement about something
Materials used, in order of use	Sequence of related statements about the topic	Series of events in chronological order
Series of steps in chronological order	Concluding statement	Concluding statement

PROCEDURE

1. The student or students select a comic sequence and read each frame.

2. Each piece is then discussed and placed in the correct sequence to reconstruct a meaningful comic story.

3. If students are working on their own, they can ask a peer to check if their comic strip is arranged correctly.

4. Alternatively, the back of each frame can be numbered, making this activity self-correcting.

PURPOSE

- Using a visual text, students practice the skills of sequencing and reading for meaning.

OVERVIEW

Individual students or a small group can use this activity. Students reconstruct cut-up comic story texts into their correct sequence.

MATERIALS

- Comic strips or comic pages cut into individual frames and laminated for durability

- Envelopes or plastic bags for storing each story sequence

▲
Sequencing a comic strip brings some smiles while the meaning is established

Working to prepare a ▶ new story for an old comic book

PURPOSE

- To encourage students to express their ideas through the medium of paint as a rehearsal for writing.

OVERVIEW

Students are given the opportunity to paint prior to writing. This encourages them to think carefully about specific details and descriptions they may wish to include in their written work.

MATERIALS

- Selection of paints or other colorful art materials
- Good quality paper
- Paper that has been divided into sections, should students wish to use this format

PROCEDURE

- Students who have successfully completed pictures and follow-up writing share their work with the rest of the class.
- The students' paintings and written work are displayed around the room.
- The teacher models his/her own painting and written work, explaining the thinking processes that were used to achieve the end result.

This is an example of linking painting and writing after the student had worked on a tile design. It is part of a unit of work in which students were asked to design different materials and fabrics.

My Tile Painting, by Sarah

I made and designed a tile. I used many colors because I wanted my tile to be attractive and bright. I have designed my tile to be a floor tile in a child's room. I think tiles like this would make a room very cheerful and happy. I am now going to work on a design for curtains for the same room.

Above is the student's edited version of what she is shown working on in the photograph.

PROCEDURE

The teacher will have previously modeled for the students how to identify textual features of a story. This activity is made more relevant by using the students' own artwork.

1. Individual students can carry out this activity, but the discussion generated in a small group helps clarify both the sequencing and identifying of specific textual features.

2. The textual features are framed as questions to encourage discussion and justification of responses.

3. The students begin by sequencing the pictures and then match the chunks of text to the textual features.

EXTENSION

As an extension of this activity, invite the group to think of alternative complications and resolutions. Innovations on the text can be carried out orally or as a written follow-up activity. This reinforces the importance of writing a narrative with the correct textual features.

Narrative Map

Title, Author, Illustrator

Setting or orientation

Characters (main and supporting)

Events

Complication/s

Resolution/s

Name:

PURPOSE

- To demonstrate to students that language is flexible and can be manipulated to link in a meaningful way to illustrations.

OVERVIEW

Students will arrange in correct sequence a series of their own pictures from a known text. They will then match chunks of texts to the pictures while identifying the textual features of this piece of writing.

MATERIALS

- Artwork from students depicting certain parts of the story

- Chunks of text typed onto individual cards that, when put in order, contain the sequence of the story

- Individual cards that depict the textual features of the writing

  For example:

  – Orientation: Who? When? Where?

  – Complication: What goes wrong?

  – Problem: What is the real problem?

  – Resolution: How is the problem solved?

PURPOSE

- To encourage students to summarize information sequentially, drawing on prior knowledge of text to complete a retell.

OVERVIEW

Students demonstrate their knowledge of sentence structure to make meaning by completing each other's sentences.

Story ladders provide opportunities for students to practice using writing conventions without having to invent the plot. They also provide an opportunity for collaborative retelling, supporting students who may have difficulty sequencing whole texts.

MATERIALS

- Writing materials

PROCEDURE

1. After hearing, reading, or viewing a story (e.g., after a guided reading session), each member of the group lists the main events in the story, deleting the last part of each sentence.

2. Students trade lists with each other and try to complete a sentence from another student's list.

3. Continue trading lists until all sentences are complete.

4. Each student shares his or her original list with the other members of the group.

VARIATION

1. Each student begins a written retelling of a story, writing one sentence.

2. Each student then trades his or her sentence and continues the retell, building on the previous sentence.

3. Students continue to trade after each new sentence is added, until the retell is complete.

4. Each student reads his or her original sentence and the collaborative retell that has evolved.

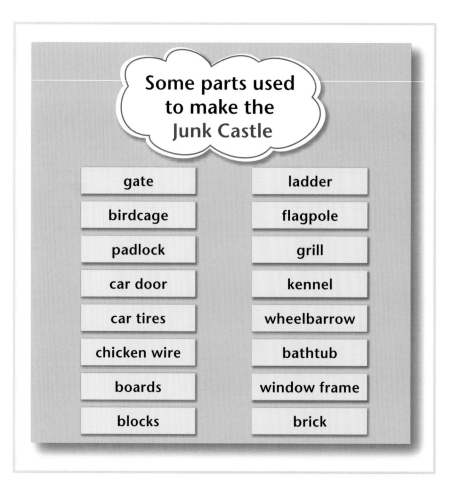

PROCEDURE

It is vital that students have been involved in the modeling and sharing of story maps with the teacher prior to their inclusion as a literacy center activity.

1. Students identify the main features of a familiar text, including setting, characters, actions, and events.

2. Plan a sequence to represent these.

3. Consider layout and decide how features will be represented, e.g., drawings, symbols, amount of written text, and pathways to direct the reader.

4. Alternatively, a story map organizer could be used.

5. Complete the story map.

6. Share the story map with others.

7. Self-evaluate the effectiveness of the story map from an audience's perspective.

When creating cooperative story maps, students could self-evaluate their skills in working collaboratively, e.g., expressing their own opinions, respecting other's ideas, taking turns, assisting others, including others, staying on task, sharing materials, and managing time.

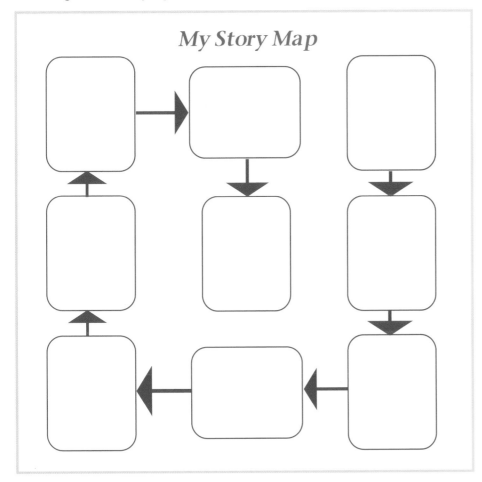

PURPOSE

- Creating story maps helps students develop their understanding of a story's structure, setting, and sequencing time. An understanding of narrative structures is, therefore, a prerequisite to the completion of a story map in the context of a literacy center.

OVERVIEW

Developing story maps provides opportunities for students to:

- develop mapping concepts

- identify major features of texts read, heard, or viewed

- retell texts in sequence

- consider audience and devise logical methods to distinguish the reader's path

- make decisions about the level of complexity of added text in order to provide clarity for the reader

Working in pairs or small groups creates opportunities for enhancement of interpersonal communication skills and supports the development of cooperative working environments.

Developing collaborative story maps creates opportunities to:

- share opinions

- make cooperative decisions with regard to layout and content

- demonstrate social skills

- problem solve

MATERIALS

- A variety of writing and drawing materials

- Familiar text

PURPOSE

- To enhance comprehension at word, sentence, and whole text level.

OVERVIEW

Using multiple copies of a short text, the students predict, recall, organize, and summarize information.

MATERIALS

- Multiple copies of a short text that can be read in about ten minutes
- Paper and writing implements

PROCEDURE

1. The teacher or the group leader reads the text title, and the students are asked to write a short sentence predicting a number of things they expect to find in the text.

2. Each group member then shares his or her responses.

3. Students are then given a copy of the text and read it independently, thinking about the predictions they made. Students may reread the text or parts of it during this time.

4. The text is then put to one side while the students write their interpretations of the text. The emphasis at this stage is for students to work quickly without referring to the text.

5. After about ten minutes, students share their interpretations and compare versions.

6. Discussion takes place about similarities and differences in the group. These can be shared during whole class sharing time or readers' circle.

7. The teacher or group leader would introduce the title of this short story and give the name of the author. If the students have read other stories by this author, discussion could take place about the style of writing, etc. The teacher or group leader would then show the drawings contained in the story. Students then take about five minutes to quickly write down what they think the story will be about. Responses could be in note form, such as:

   - a bridge and a storm

   - somebody drowning

   - helping somebody in trouble

   - a flood

8. The students then share their responses and read the story silently. Once the reading has been completed, students are asked to summarize the story in four or five sentences without referring to the text. Then they share their summarizing and also which of their predictions were closest to the story.

◄ **Retelling the text**

PROCEDURE

Students work individually or in pairs.

1. Provide text pieces only to begin with.

2. Students read all text pieces.

3. Discuss and identify the genre.

4. Construct the text, taking into account generic structure and cohesiveness.

5. Once this has been done, the group compares the text they have constructed with a copy of the complete text.

6. Identify and discuss any differences in the sequencing of the pieces. Justify decisions made.

EXTENSION

1. Follow steps 1 to 4 above.

2. Identify ways in which the text could be improved.

3. Edit the text, using the writing materials provided.

4. Leave the text for teacher evaluation.

5. Exclude the use of the complete text for comparison.

EXAMPLE

If a group of students wrote a report based on a reading of *Butterflies & Moths*, a teacher could use their report to consolidate the genre of report writing by cutting it into the appropriate sections and having cards describing each section of the report, as shown below. (*Butterflies & Moths* is written by Graham Meadows and Claire Vial, and is published by Dominie Press.)

PURPOSE

- To analyze text and identify the genre in which it is written.

OVERVIEW

Students manipulate pieces of text to demonstrate understanding of the impact of text structure and sequence on text cohesion.

MATERIALS

- Use a variety of texts written by students. These have been cut into sentences or paragraphs. When preparing texts, copy individual texts on different colored pieces of paper for ease of identification.

- A complete copy of the text

- Writing materials (for the extension task)

- The genre of the text, level of text difficulty, and ability of the students will determine how the texts are cut.

| Butterflies and Moths | Name the genre | Report |

| Butterflies and moths are insects that have wings covered with tiny, individually colored scales that form beautiful patterns and designs. There are about 160,000 species of butterflies and moths. | Title | Purpose – presenting factual information about something by classifying characteristics. |

Most butterflies fly during the day, but moths fly at dusk or at night. Butterflies appear in many beautiful colors, but moths are a dull color.

Butterflies and moths live all over the world, except in Antarctica. They are most often found in tropical rainforests, but they also live in dry deserts, high mountains, pastures, and marshes.

Related statements about the topic

Butterflies and moths are very important because they pollinate flowers. And caterpillars are important in the food chain. But caterpillars can be pests, too, when they eat farmers' crops and the plants in people's gardens.

Opening general statement

Concluding statement

SEMANTIC GRID

PURPOSE

- Students will learn how to match a set of attributes to a particular concept.

OVERVIEW

Students use a graphic organizer to develop the skills of identifying details and comparing properties or concepts from informational texts.

MATERIALS

- An informational text
- A grid with the concepts listed in the left-hand column and the descriptors along the top row

PROCEDURE

1. Model and demonstrate the use of the grid prior to students working individually or in small groups.

2. The information from the text is set out as shown. The page number that substantiates the information can also be added to the appropriate box.

3. Once students become familiar with this process, they can be encouraged to design and complete their own semantic grids.

Travel	Wheels	Wings	Uses fuel	Engine	Carries passengers
Cars					
Walking					
Boat					
Bike					
Airplane					
Bus					
Train					
Helicopter					
Seaplane					

Graphic organizer for comparing properties

PROCEDURE

A number of authentic contexts for sentence manipulation activities can be provided, including shared texts, individual written excerpts, texts from oral reports and news reports. Sentence manipulations can be used by individuals, small groups, or a whole class.

Whole class manipulations provide an opportunity to model the variety of manipulations and explicitly teach the impact that manipulation has on the structure and the meaning of a sentence.

Word choices can be made from a variety of sources, including word banks, favorite texts, special events, oral recounts, dictionaries, and thesauruses.

TYPES OF SENTENCE MANIPULATIONS

Simple sentence making

Students construct sentences using a variety of sources to stimulate word choices. Sentences can be constructed one word at a time using individual word cards. Alternatively, the sentence can be written on a sentence strip and cut into individual word and punctuation cards, and then reconstructed to form the complete sentence.

In our hard-working class, we do our best to help others.

Sentence expansion

Extend an existing sentence by inserting additional words (e.g., adjectives, adverbs), phrases, and clauses. In this way, children learn to make more complex sentences, e.g., using conjunctions.

It was a nice day, so we went to the park.

Tuesday dawned the most beautiful sunny day, so we decided we should take advantage of the fine weather and walk to the local park.

Sentence reduction

Reduce a longer sentence to its simplest form. Students could also reduce two or more sentences to make one sentence, focusing on maintaining meaning. This is a more difficult task than sentence expansion, as students are required to reread and make decisions about relevant information required to ensure meaning is maintained.

We went to the beach and went swimming and played a game of volleyball and it was good and then it got late we went home to watch TV.

All day we had lots of fun playing on the beach but when it got late we went home.

Sentence transformation

Manipulate the sentence, changing one word at a time. Grammatical

PURPOSE

- To demonstrate to students that language is flexible and can be manipulated in a variety of ways, and still make sense.

OVERVIEW

Students are given different sentence structures and are required to change, improve, complete, or transform them in some way.

MATERIALS

- Sentence strips
- Word cards
- Scissors
- Sentence maker or pocket chart (optional)
- Photocopied sections of text on cards
- White board

structures must be maintained, e.g., substituting a verb for a verb. Transformations enable children to decide on changes to sentence structures that are necessary when grammatical features in the sentence change, e.g., singular to plural participants or a change in tense.

> The old man walked down the street looking very sad and lonely.

> An elderly male wandered along the pavement. His appearance showed that he was unhappy and alone.

Matching sentence parts

Multiple sentences from a text are cut into individual word cards and jumbled up. Students are required to reconstruct the sentences to make a cohesive text. Alternatively, sentences could be cut into phrases or clauses and reconstructed to make complete sentences in order to reconstruct the text.

Sentence completion

Provide the students with a variety of sentence beginnings or endings, cut into individual words. They are required to invent the missing parts. The use of conjunctions (*if, but, therefore, although, unless*, etc.) provides an added level of difficulty.

> I ride my bike

> My mom gets mad

> I watch TV

> When I get tired

> I go to school

> My best friend

> Today I was late

Sentence modeling

Model sentence patterns from a familiar or shared text to form the basis for the construction of more sentences.

Sentence comparison

Compare sentences constructed by students to retell a story or piece of text with those contained in the actual story or text. This provides a focus for discussion on the impact of word order on meaning and reader appeal.

◄ **Sorting jumbled word cards**

STUDENT WRITING

The story began with Damien being caught in a big storm. He was trying to get home, and he was cold.

ACTUAL TEXT

The cold sleet flattened his yellow raincoat against his body and dribbled down his right leg. Half his face was whipped by the driving wind, his hat flapped wildly over his ear, his hands were as cold as snow, but he was not aware of any of this ...

Sentence stems

Students are presented with sentence stems and are required to change words in order to enhance meaning.

Sports activity day was coming soon.

The whole school anxiously awaited the arrival of sports activity day, and excitement was high.

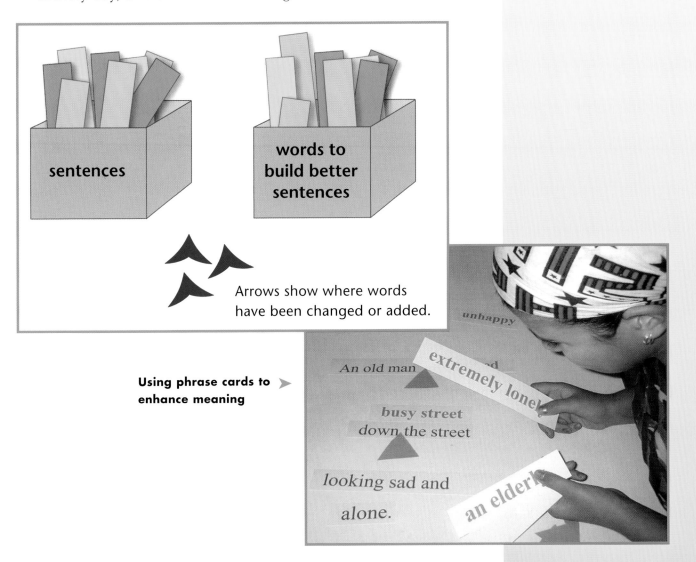

sentences

words to build better sentences

Arrows show where words have been changed or added.

Using phrase cards to enhance meaning ▶

unhappy

An old man extremely lonely

busy street

down the street

looking sad and

alone.

an elderly

TEXT GRAMMAR

PURPOSE

- To help students identify and organize grammatical information from a text.

OVERVIEW

Students use a text to identify parts of grammar in the text and record their answers on a form.

MATERIALS

- Text grammar form
- Writing materials
- Text (optional)

PROCEDURE

Prior to use in a literacy center, the teacher and students brainstorm to compile headings that suit the particular text types.

It is important that the use of the text grammar form is modeled with the class or group prior to its use in a literacy center.

1. Students select details from the story and write them under the appropriate headings on the form.

2. Students complete the task with text support or from memory without the text.

EXAMPLE

This example of a text grammar form is based on a reading of *Lookout Boy*, written by Elizabeth Van Steenwyk, and published by Dominie Press.

Text Grammar

Title
Lookout Boy

Setting
the docks
San Francisco
Uncle Zeb's store
lookout hill
edge of the hill
the harbor
edge of the cliff
the middle of a field

Character Description

David Jenkins — Persistent, good-natured boy, determined to be a lookout boy.

Uncle Zeb — David's uncle, store owner, kind, protective.

Silas — One of the older lookout boys. Teases David, but gives him credit for spotting the fire.

John — One of the lookout boys. Also teases David, but credits him in the end.

Joe — A lookout boy who joined in the teasing but praised David for saving the town.

Name:

References to Time

May, 1851
every week
next year
all day long
tomorrow
the next day
now
a minute ago
a few days
the next day
most of the time
an hour
every day
every minute

Events and Actions

David stood on the docks.
He walked downtown to Uncle Zeb's store.
David talked with Uncle Zeb about becoming a lookout boy.
The older boys teased David and took his lunch pail.
The older boys took David's spyglass.
David played a trick on one of the older boys.
The older boys rested in the shade of a tree, but there was no room for David.
David spotted a ship, but it was a garbage scow.
David spotted a curl of smoke in the middle of the field.
David tried to wake the older boys.
David told Uncle Zeb and the others about the fire.
Everybody worked hard to save the town.
Uncle Zeb thanked the boys for helping to save the town.
The older lookout boys gave David credit and said he was a great lookout boy.

Complication and Resolution

The older boys teased David, but when he played a trick on Silas, they stopped. Everybody said David was too little to be a lookout boy, but when he spotted a fire and warned the town, they said he was the very best.

PROCEDURE

1. Most students are familiar with the game of bingo. Explain that the group will take turns to be the caller. This means that one student in the group reads out the words on the individual cards.

2. Students then identify which aspect of a text this word or phrase represents.

3. If the students have this aspect on their bingo cards, they place a counter on top of the word.

4. The first person to place counters on all nine spaces can call out "Bingo."

5. This person is then the caller for the next game.

6. The individual cards are shuffled, and students can exchange cards.

EXAMPLE OF BINGO BOARD

Author	Illustrator	Spine
Biography	Title	Blurb

EXAMPLES OF CALLER CARDS

J.K. Rowling	Animalia	Born in England in 1958, Graeme Base graduated from art school in 1978. His books have sold over 30,000 copies.

Using text bingo to identify specific parts of a text

PURPOSE

• To develop the skill of identifying, naming, and understanding specific parts of a text.

OVERVIEW

By using the format of the game bingo, students learn to recognize the components of texts.

MATERIALS

• A bingo card for each member of the group (4–6 students). Each card should be different, although some words may be repeated.

• A series of cards with a word or phrase that represents part of a text.

For example:

– the name of or information about an author

– the title of a book

– the name of a character

– information about a character

– blurbs about a text

– a container of small counters

PURPOSE

- To identify and comprehend components of a text at sentence level.

OVERVIEW

Using sentences from a familiar text and the format of *Who? What? Where?* and *Why?* students arrange the sentences under each of the headings.

MATERIALS

- Laminated chart divided into four columns with the headings: *Who? What? Where? Why?*

- Sentences from a familiar text cut into components of sentence structure (words and phrases)

- White board markers or wet erase pens

PROCEDURE

1. Reconstruct the sentences so that they are structurally correct. To complete this, students will have to draw on their knowledge of the text.

2. Identify the components of each sentence and write the appropriate word or phrase under one of the headings.

SAMPLE OF A CLASSROOM CHART TO ASSIST STUDENTS WITH IDENTIFYING COMPONENTS OF A TEXT AT SENTENCE LEVEL

At the beach the two boys swam far out to sea because they thought it would be fun.

PROCEDURE

As with all literacy center activities, semantic overviews require modeling and demonstration prior to students working independently, either in a group or individually.

1. Students read a chapter of a book or an article.

2. Discussion then takes place as to the most important piece of information in the text. In order to do this, students have to make judgments about the author's purpose.

3. At first a teacher would need to model the questioning in ways that support the students. For example, "What message do you think the author is trying to get us to think about?"

4. The main idea is then placed in the top frame and students decide on the supporting ideas for the main idea. These are again recorded and then any other relevant information is added to the last set of frames.

EXAMPLE OF A NARRATIVE SEMANTIC OVERVIEW

Falling (a short narrative by Goldie Alexander, from *Thrills and Spills*, published by Longman).

- Main idea – Scott's fear of heights and how he overcame this fear.

- Supporting ideas – Scott's acceptance of his mother's new partner.

- A trip to the mountain that went wrong.

- The change in the relationship and Scott's feeling when there was danger.

- Other relevant facts – Scott's mother was very proud of him.

- The beginning of a new relationship between Scott and Keith.

EXAMPLE OF A NON-NARRATIVE SEMANTIC OVERVIEW

Living Fossils, by Joanne Sinclair (from *Amazing Nature*, published by Longman).

- Main idea – Although some fossils are millions of years old, some of the creatures are still alive today.

- Supporting ideas/information – Many paleontologists are still finding living examples of fossils that are millions of years old.

- Fossils are found all over the world.

- Fossils can be shells, insects, fish, or animals.

- Other relevant information – The living fossils that have survived have done so because they are adaptable to the environment.

PURPOSE

- To develop the skill of linking new information to prior knowledge and to extract the main ideas from a text structure.

Note: A text structure is an organizational pattern or framework used by the author. There are narrative story structures and non-narrative story structures.

OVERVIEW

Using multiple copies of a text, students discuss, locate, and record the main idea, supporting ideas, and other relevant information. This approach also forms the basis for note taking.

MATERIALS

- Multiple copies of a text

- Large sheet of paper to record group findings or individual graphic outline

WORD BUILDING

PURPOSE

- To encourage students to extend their knowledge of words.

OVERVIEW

By manipulating letters and clusters of letters, students are able to make lists of words and word families.

MATERIALS

- Cards with small words written on them
- Cards with single letters or blends written on them
- It is helpful if these two sets of cards are prepared in two different colors.

PROCEDURE

1. The small word cards are placed face down.

2. In pairs or a small group, one student chooses a card and places it face up.

3. The next student picks up a letter card and, if possible, adds it to the small word. If this is not possible, the student replaces the card. The aim is for the pair or group to extend the small words wherever possible.

   For example:

   | g | at | e | s |

4. The pairs or groups of students see how many extended words they can make in a given amount of time.

Individual students can also work with this resource to improve word-building skills.

Other resources that can be used in a word building center are:

- letter tiles

- magnetic letters

▲
Word building in a small group

PROCEDURE

In pairs, students place the correct word card next to a correct prefix or suffix.

Choose the right prefix

dis | like
un
re
mis
ex
anti

just

biotic

turn

lead

gravity

plain   taken

known

most

mother

week

Choose the right suffix

assist | ant
ful
ly
er
est
less

teach

bright

mouth

pain

EXTENSION

Once words have been placed alongside the prefix or suffix, students can:

- check the spelling of the word in a dictionary

- write definitions of the word created

- read around the room or look in a text to locate words that begin or end with the same prefix or suffix

Classroom prefix and suffix charts can be interactive, with students adding to charts as they find new words.

PURPOSE

- To match words with an appropriate prefix or suffix.

OVERVIEW

By manipulating words with suitable prefixes and suffixes, students become familiar with this word-building strategy.

MATERIALS

- Cards with prefixes or suffixes written down the side

- Word cards

PURPOSE

Students will understand the importance of phonograms (a letter cluster that begins with a vowel) in assisting them to decode and spell a wide variety of words.

MATERIALS

- Sentence holder or pocket chart

- Selection of phonograms on cards

- Use individual alphabet letters or beginning word blends. These can be color-coded, as shown in the illustration, to support students' learning.

PROCEDURE

- Demonstrate and model how many words can by made by placing the phonograms in list format and then adding a beginning letter or letter blend (see example below).

- Students then see how many words they can form, using the selection of phonograms provided.

- As they work through this process, they will see that each list they have made rhymes.

- Students can then use the words to make their own nonsense poems.

r	pr	str	m	k

take	ight	ould	ing
make			
rake			
stake			
drake			

An example of a poem following the above activity.

High Utility Phonograms

ack	at	ill	ore
ail	ate	in	ot
ain	aw	ine	uck
ake	ay	ing	ug
ale	eat	ink	ump
ame	est	ip	unk
an	ice	it	ilk
ank	ick	ock	
ap	ode	oke	
ash	ight	op	

I went out at night
The moon was so bright
I did not need a light.

Adam, Grade 3

Focusing on phonograms ➤

PROCEDURE

Building words, using given clues. In the examples below, the focus changes from individual letters in the first example to demonstrating an understanding of syllables in the second.

EXAMPLE 1

I can fly.

My first letter is in *peas* but not in *seas.*

My second letter is the letter before *b.*

My third letter is in *rain, tear,* and *for.*

My fourth letter is the same as my third.

My fifth letter is the letter between *n* and *p.*

My sixth letter is in *tease* but not *please.*

What am I?

Answer: A parrot.

EXAMPLE 2

Make a three-syllable word beginning with *c.*

My first syllable rhymes with *Tom.*

My second (middle) syllable rhymes with *you.*

My third (last) syllable rhymes with *her.*

What am I?

Answer: A computer.

EXTENSION

Students could work individually or in pairs to develop word puzzles for others to solve.

PURPOSE

- Word puzzles can take many forms and provide opportunities for students to play with words, and thus explore language.

- Word puzzles engage students in problem-solving activities, enabling them to analyze and monitor language as they develop their understandings about spelling, and of how language works.

OVERVIEW

Students build words from prepared cards that give clues as to which letters are required to make a word. In the examples given, the focus changes from individual letters in the first example to demonstrating an understanding of syllables in the second.

MATERIALS

- Writing materials
- Word building cards

PURPOSE

- To enable students to locate small words contained in larger words, which is a necessary skill in both reading and writing.

OVERVIEW

The teacher provides the students with laminated cards that have several large words clearly written along the first row. Students identify as many small words as they can from the larger words.

MATERIALS

- Laminated cards with three or four large words displayed
- Dictionaries
- Whiteboard markers or wet erase pens

PROCEDURE

Demonstrate first with a whole class before you have the students work on their own, in pairs, or in small groups.

1. Show students how they need to locate smaller words and write them in the space below.

2. Students must then use their dictionaries to ascertain that they are finding real words.

3. It is important to stress that the letters of the smaller words must be kept in the same order as they are in the large words.

4. When students have completed their cards, they can compare them with their peers and see if any words can be added.

A format for the cards is shown below.

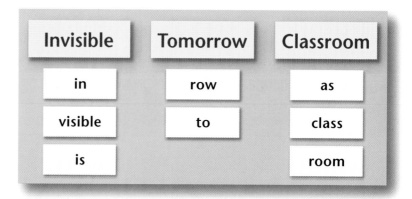

Invisible	Tomorrow	Classroom
in	row	as
visible	to	class
is		room

Locating small words in a larger word

PROCEDURE

Students can make personal word webs or develop them in small groups.

1. The beginning word may be chosen by an individual or a group, or alternatively, the teacher may provide a word related to a text, topic, or concept.

2. The type of associated words to record may be decided by students, or provided by the teacher.

3. The beginning word is placed in the center of the page. Spokes are used, with associated words recorded around the central word.

4. A box of "words" and "ways to think about words" could be provided, with one card being drawn from each box to create the word web.

5. Word webs can be interactive because, once they are started and displayed on cards in the room, others can add spokes as words are discovered.

6. Students can use a dictionary to locate word derivations.

Word derivations:

(demonstrating etymological knowledge)

aerodynamic

aerobatics

aerosol

aero

aeronautical

aerobics

aerospace

PURPOSE

- Word webs help students make word associations. They also encourage them to make connections in solving words when they read and write.

OVERVIEW

Word web activities may include word associations related to:

- words that rhyme

- words that have similar letter patterns

- words with common sounds

- words that end with the same suffix

- compound words

- words that begin with the same prefix

- words that mean the same thing or have a similar meaning (synonyms)

- words with the same root origins (etymological knowledge)

- etymological word webs assist students to understand how word origins affect meaning and spelling patterns

MATERIALS

A variety of materials can be used to record word webs:

- felt pens and paper (a variety of sizes and colors)

- whiteboard markers and whiteboards

- chalk and chalkboards

- paint and paper

- wet erase pens and film

INDEPENDENT READING CENTER

WRITING CENTER

These icons can be reproduced without permission from the publisher.

COMPUTER CENTER

RESPONDING TO TEXT CENTER

These icons can be reproduced without permission from the publisher.

CRITICAL LITERACY CENTER

GENRE CENTER

These icons can be reproduced without permission from the publisher.

SEQUENCING AND RETELLING CENTER

TEXT STRUCTURE CENTER

These icons can be reproduced without permission fr

WORD STUDY CENTER